CHILDREN IN CRISIS

THE MIDDLE EAST

Struggle for a Homeland

Photos by John Isaac
Text by
Keith Greenberg

j953
GRE

A BLACKBIRCH PRESS BOOK

WOODBRIDGE, CONNECTICUT

Published by Blackbirch Press, Inc.
260 Amity Road
Woodbridge, CT 06525
©1997 Blackbirch Press, Inc.

First Edition

Printed in the United States of America

10 9 8 7 6 5 4 3 2 1

Photo credits on page 32

Library of Congress Cataloging-in-Publication Data
Isaac, John.
  Middle East: struggle for a homeland/photos by John Isaac; text by Keith Greenberg.—1st ed.
      p.   cm. — (Children in crisis)
  Includes bibliographical references and index.
  Summary: Explores the human side of the conflict in the Middle East, a land torn apart by violence.
    ISBN 1-56711-187-4 (lib. bdg. : alk. paper)
    1. Gaza Strip—Juvenile literature. 2. Jewish–Arab relations—1949—Juvenile literature. [1. Gaza Strip. 2. Jewish–Arab relations.]
          I. Greenberg, Keith Elliot. II. Title. III. Series.
          DS110.G3I83   1997
          953'.1—dc20
                                                                96-1230
                                                                CIP
                                                                AC

Opposite: Palestinian children wander through the hills of south Lebanon.

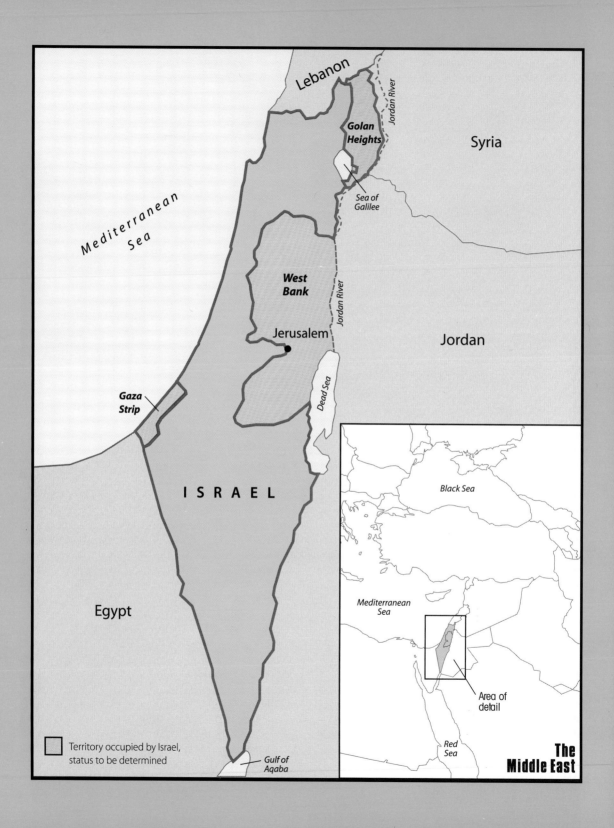

Lebanon

Golan
Heights

Jordan River

Syria

Mediterranean
Sea

Sea of
Galilee

West
Bank

Jordan River

Jerusalem

Jordan

Gaza
Strip

Dead Sea

ISRAEL

Egypt

Black Sea

Mediterranean
Sea

Area of
detail

Red
Sea

Territory occupied by Israel,
status to be determined

Gulf of
Aqaba

**The
Middle East**

A LOOK AT
THE MIDDLE EAST

People have been fighting over the area known as Palestine since biblical days. The area's borders have also shifted over time. Today, the region is divided between land that is controlled by Israel and land that is controlled by Palestinian authorities. Israelis and Palestinians have battled each other for many years. In 1993, the two sides signed a truce after nearly five decades of war. As they continue to work out the details of the agreement, the exact boundaries of the region are still unclear. No one can say exactly where Israel ends and Palestine begins.

The area called Palestine is located in the Middle East, on the east coast of the Mediterranean Sea. The land contains hills, mountains, and desert. Because of its many holy sites, the city of Jerusalem in Israel has special meaning to both Israelis and Palestinians. Although Israel rules Jerusalem now, many Palestinians hope to one day govern at least part of the city.

In the 14th century B.C., two forces invaded the land. One group was a collection of Hebrew tribes. They would later adopt the Jewish religion, and call the area "Israel." The others were known as the Philistines. The word *Palestine* would be based on their name. Their descendants are Arabs— some Muslim, some Christian.

Three of the world's most important religions took shape in Jerusalem. Jews built temples there. The followers of Jesus Christ—a Jewish scholar who preached in the city—broke away from the Jewish religion and started Christianity. According to Muslim belief, Muhammed, the founder of the Islamic faith, rose to heaven from Jerusalem in the 7th century.

The Turks took over Palestine in 1517. They held it until World War I, when the British captured the area. Most of the country was Palestinian then, but the situation was quickly changing. Adolf Hitler soon took power in Germany, and vowed to rid the world of Jews. Seeing no place else to run, European Jews fled to Palestine—their homeland during Biblical times. The Palestinians feared that the newcomers would take their land. There were several riots between the two groups.

Left: Beirut, Lebanon.
Above: A worshiper leaves the sacred Dome of the Rock in Jerusalem.
Below: Jews pray at Jerusalem's Western Wall, or Wailing Wall.

A group of Palestinian refugee children stands in line waiting for food in Jordan.

In 1947, the British planned to leave Palestine. The United Nations proposed the creation of two countries—one Jewish and one Arab. The Jews accepted the plan, but the Palestinians objected. Their leaders said it wasn't fair that the Jews would receive 56 percent of the territory, even though they were only one third of the population.

On May 14, 1948, Israel declared itself an independent Jewish state. Five Arab nations immediately attacked the new country. The Arabs claimed that they were coming to the aid of the Palestinians. Israel won the war, and took territory that was originally supposed to be part of the Palestinian homeland. The area that Israel didn't capture was swallowed up by other Arab countries. Jordan occupied the West Bank of the Jordan River. Egypt claimed the Gaza Strip.

The Palestinians were left with nothing. About 780,000 became homeless. Many moved to other Arab states.

In 1967, Israel and its Arab neighbors went to war again. This time, the Israelis seized the West Bank from Jordan and the Gaza Strip from Egypt—areas that Palestinians had considered home. An additional 500,000 Palestinians became refugees. Some remained in areas controlled by Israel—called the "occupied territories." There, Palestinians and Israelis were in constant conflict. One Arab uprising—called the "intifada"—started in 1987 and lasted for several years.

JOHN'S STORY

The first time I traveled to the Middle East, I thought of my father. He was a minister in a small town in southern India called Trichy. And the Bible was a big part of our lives.

It was in Palestine, in the ancient city of Jericho, that I saw an old shepherd leading sheep down a hill. I wished my father could be standing there with me. This was the land of his Bible stories. I felt like I'd gone back in time.

As a photographer working for the United Nations (UN), I had come to the Middle East because of the troubles there. During several wars with Israel, many Palestinians had been driven off their land. The Palestine Liberation Organization (PLO) was a military-style group dedicated to Palestinian independence. Members of the PLO settled near the Israeli border, in south Lebanon. Violent battles between the PLO and the Israeli Army were common.

UN photographer John Isaac took this picture of the old city of Jericho.

A UN peacekeeper guides a helicopter in for a landing in south Lebanon.

In 1978, Israel invaded south Lebanon. The United Nations sent soldiers to the region. The purpose of the UN force was to keep the two sides apart. UN workers provided food, clothing, and medicine for Palestinian families. They also built schools for the children.

Soon Lebanon was in the middle of a civil war between Lebanese Christians and Muslims. The PLO was siding with the Muslims. The Israelis were supporting the Christians. Beirut, Lebanon's capital, had once been considered the most beautiful city in the Middle East. By 1979, however, it was heavily damaged by the fierce fighting.

Left: Downtown Beirut was destroyed by the fighting during the 1970s.
Below: Palestinian youths make friends with a UN soldier in Lebanon.

Everywhere I went, I saw how war had ruined people's lives.

Palestinians who lived on the border of Israel had fled to Beirut. There weren't any homes for them there, so families lived on the golf course.

Farmers had abandoned their orange groves. Sometimes, I would pick the oranges off the tree before they rotted, and eat them. But I had to be careful. Land mines had been planted in some orange groves. If I had stepped on one, it would have exploded.

Opposite: Palestinian refugees in Beirut were forced to live in makeshift camps.

On my way to south Lebanon, I met an old Palestinian couple whose house had been destroyed. All they had left were family photos and a beat-up blue chair. As I spoke to them, the woman said, "I have to make you tea."

"Why?" I asked her.

"Because you're in my house. We Arabs believe that we should always treat our guests with hospitality."

"But there's no house left," I argued.

The woman picked through the rubble. Finally, she made a strong triangle out of three stones. She placed paper and wood chips in the middle and started a small fire. Then she made me mint tea.

A south Lebanon couple search through the rubble of what had been their home.

   One of the most upsetting parts of my assignment was seeing the effect of war on children. I saw boys not older than 14, in military uniforms, ready to fight. In America, they'd be playing football or studying for their exams. Here, they were preparing to go to war.

   Two years after my first visit, I flew back to south Lebanon. The United Nations had sent troops there from many countries. I met soldiers from Senegal, Sweden, France, Nepal, Ireland, and Ghana, among other countries. All of them wore blue helmets—the symbol of UN peacekeepers. But there was still a great deal of conflict between the Palestinians and the Israelis.

Opposite: UN forces roll into south Lebanon.
Right: Palestinian brothers read together in Jordan.
Below: A mother and daughter wait together at the Souf camp in Jordan.

One of the most interesting regiments was from Fiji, a small country in the South Pacific. These kind soldiers were mostly tall and muscular, and many had big mustaches. I saw the Fijians bring water to people who didn't have any. They also rebuilt schools, churches, and mosques. When they marched through town, they wore exotic outfits. It was easy for me to understand why the Palestinian children were fascinated by them.

Nobody liked the Fijians more than Salah. He was a nine-year-old whose parents had been killed in the fighting. Even though his life had been so tough, he still had a sense of humor. He'd make the Fijian soldiers laugh by teasing them about their long mustaches.

Below and opposite: Salah enjoys the company of Fijian peacekeepers in his hometown in south Lebanon.

When the soldiers rode through town, Salah sat in the colonel's jeep. He would tell jokes in a gruff voice and pick up everyone's spirits.

The Fijian soldiers stayed in Lebanon for only a short period of time. When a new unit came to the Middle East, there was a colorful parade. Salah would usually watch, sitting on top of a soldier's shoulders.

This was the type of kid who could survive anywhere. I knew that—no matter how much danger he faced—he'd find success.

Salah rides with Fijian colonel Sandy Qana through the countryside of south Lebanon.

In September 1993, a major breakthrough in peace occurred. Israeli prime minister Yitzhak Rabin signed a treaty with Palestine Liberation Organization leader Yasir Arafat in Washington, D.C. As President Bill Clinton and the rest of the world watched, the two old enemies shook hands. They agreed to end their conflict once and for all.

The peace agreement called for many changes. Among them was the release of certain areas to the Palestinians. One day, the Palestinians hope to have a fully independent homeland.

U.S. president Bill Clinton (center) presided over the historic signing of the peace treaty in 1993. Yitzhak Rabin (left) and Yasir Arafat (right) shook hands after the agreement was signed.

Despite these great achievements, peace in the Middle East remains uncertain. There is still much work and much struggle left to go. Extremists on both sides of the struggle are not happy with the peace agreement that has been generally accepted. Certain people on both sides want all the land to themselves.

In November 1995, the peace process was dealt a serious blow. It was then that Yitzhak Rabin was assassinated by an Israeli who hoped to shatter the truce. In February and March 1996, more tragedy struck, when a series of bombings against Israel killed 57 people and wounded hundreds. For many people, these bombings also exploded any hope for a real and lasting peace in the Middle East.

Even more violence threatened peace in April 1996. In reaction to the bombings of February and March, Israel launched an attack against a UN refugee camp in south Lebanon. By the time the artillery shells stopped falling, 100 people were dead. Israeli officials acknowledged that they "regretted" the action but said it was necessary to stop Lebanese guerrillas from launching rocket attacks into northern Israel. A cease-fire was called immediately.

Opposite: Wreckage from a bomb that exploded in a bus filled the street in downtown Jerusalem in 1996.

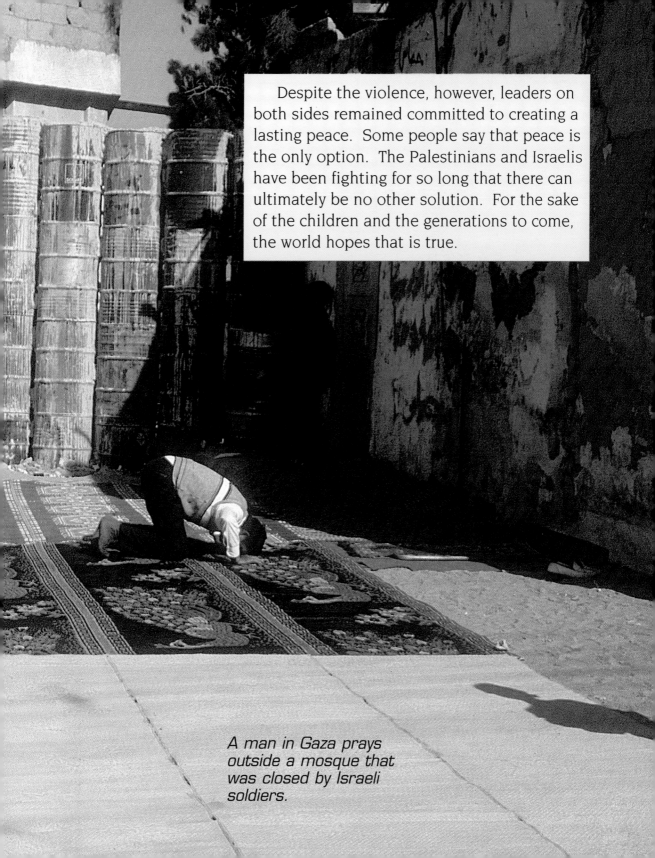

Despite the violence, however, leaders on both sides remained committed to creating a lasting peace. Some people say that peace is the only option. The Palestinians and Israelis have been fighting for so long that there can ultimately be no other solution. For the sake of the children and the generations to come, the world hopes that is true.

A man in Gaza prays outside a mosque that was closed by Israeli soldiers.

FOR FURTHER READING

Ambruster, Ann. *The United Nations*. Danbury, CT: Watts, 1995.

Gikow, Louise, & Weiss, Ellen. *For Every Child a Better World*. New York: Western, 1993.

Long, Cathryn J. *The Middle East in Search of Peace*. Brookfield, CT: The Millbrook Press, 1994.

Rogoff, Mike. *Israel*. Chatham, NJ: Raintree Steck-Vaughn, 1990.

Stefoff, Rebecca. *West Bank-Gaza Strip*. Broomall, PA: Chelsea House, 1988.

Taylor, Allegra. *A Kibbutz in Israel*. Minneapolis, MN: Lerner, 1987.

INDEX

PHOTO CREDITS